Marriage is Like Mashed Potatoes

Marriage is Like Mashed Potatoes

T.M.C. TROUBLED OR
MAINTAINING OR COMING INTO
THE MARRIAGE COVENANT
GOD HAS A WORD FOR YOU

Carol A. Overton Saunders

Hope Now Publishing
Bowie, Maryland

Copyright © 2015 by Carol A. Overton Saunders

All rights reserved. No part of this publication may be reproduced, distributed or transmitted in any form or by any means, without prior written permission.

Carol A. Overton Saunders/Hope Now Publishing Company P.O. Box 413 Bowie, MD 20718 www.carolsaundersent.com

Publisher's Note: This is a work of non-fiction, unrehearsed, undressed and uncovered Truth. This work is also a product of the author's imagination from her creative artistic background. Locales and public names are sometimes used for atmospheric purposes. Any resemblance to actual people, living or dead, or to businesses, companies, events, institutions, or locales is completely coincidental.

Book Layout © 2014 BookDesignTemplates.com

Marriage is like Mash Potatoes 1st ed. ISBN: 0692550240
ISBN 13: 9780692550243

This Book is Dedicated

⸸

To my cousin, friend and co-laborer with Jesus Christ. Minister Cecilio Gonzalez, III, POPI; who received his wings on Feb. 28, 2014. Cecilio and 3 other people, including Chief Deputy of the Garza County Sheriff's Office, stopped to help a driver of a box truck that skidded off the roadway. Another truck jackknifed and hit them. Popi, I know you are praying for your brothers and sisters who are Troubled or Maintaining or Coming into the Marriage Covenant.

Loving~ U4Life Cousin, Son, Family, Father, Husband & Servant!

Forward

First and foremost, I would like to honor this awesome amazing Woman of Excellence Mrs. Carol A. Overton Saunders for allowing me the opportunity to write this foreword.

The Lord has impregnated her with this book. You will experience her passion and fire on this topic as you begin to read these chapters. Her heart is poured on every page.

May this be the book to bring healing, restoration, inspiration and information for your relationship.

As with the potato all relationships start off raw. All potatoes must go through some heat to enjoy. The most intense would be cooked mash potatoes.

In a time when marriages are dissolving like an outdated alka seltzer dropped into water, relationships are fizzing away; love is dissolving. This is a timely piece.

All relationships experience hardships, obstacles, to conquer, overcome and defeat.

We understand that marriage is a continual process of transformation, changes, growing, making. adjustments, maturing and emerging as two become one. Preferably both finding the right way to merge themselves; good and bad, to make something valuable and precious to enjoy.

We will look at 2 people as potatoes.

The exterior is quite hard and has to be stripped of it's covering by peeling the skin off. It takes an insurmountable number of pressure painful humbling. There are various ways to cook a potato; they require some form of heat, to take it from raw form to cooked form. It's called Process. Not sure if raw potatoes would be a delight to eat. *some people wash theirs before peeling* yet the surface is still hard.

That outside skin is the first process; the skin has to be peeled off. When entering the covenant your outside skin has to be peeled, stripped of your past relationships, even from mother and father. Stripped of what previous people have done. The skin has to must be Peeled of the single attitude when you are married. Stripped of the control mentality. It then has to be cut, sliced, and diced. There are wounds that have to be cut away; some offensive things have to be cut out for the sake of a healthier marriage. It is easier to boil the potato when it is cut into sections. It then goes into heat, fire and hot water. Sometimes it will be hot other times not, the water has to reach the right temperature for boiling. You will reach boiling points in the relationship because of hot water situations you can get into * It would do good not to let things get to a boiling point, where things get escalated and begin to spill over out of pot.

Having the right recipe when you get to the boiling point will help you a lot. After the boiling, the potatoes are now drained of excess water, no residue or it will mess up the texture of the mashed potatoes. Then comes more crushing, mashing, turning and mashing; to humble, soften you up. These are the various trials of daily relationships; it is all in how you handle it.

Which brings me now to the seasoning; No one wants bland mashed potatoes. To sustain marriage, Keep God at the head at all times, He has to become your go to guy. He can handle your mate better than anyone you rely on, because He knows you both, He will teach you both, how to treat one another. Then we need a little salt to preserve it and pepper to keep it spicy, these are things that die off if you let it. Prayer, Prayer and More Prayer is a preserver along with the right speech, less you end up in hot water! Patience to endure the heat to become softened, butter is continual forgiveness which will help in this process, as you rely on God,

All the process which the potatoes go through are the hands of God mashing up something beautiful to enjoy. Love is beautiful and all the hardships make it worth going through the process.

Don't let a microwave potato and flake box potato destroy God's process of mashing you together. Yes, Marriage is like mashed potatoes.

By His Spirit World Mission
 Advancing the Kingdom with Love and a Vengeance!
 Setting the Captives Free!!! Apostle Angela D. Thomas
 www.byhispirit.org byhispirit633@gmail.com
 Not by Might, Nor by Power, but By My Spirit says the Lord of Hosts-Zech 4:6

From the Author

I ENJOY A DELICIOUS MEAL. I believe in marriage. I adore our God our Creator. I enjoy a loaded potato- pleasure. I love a beautiful garden.

Apostle Carol A. Overton Saunders

> TWO PEOPLE COME TOGETHER FULL OF EXPECTATIONS.
> THEY ALSO COME TOGETHER WITH INGREDIENTS NOT PLEASING TO GOD.
>
> THE BLOOD OF JESUS IS LIKE GRAVY POURED OVER OUR EMOTIONS, HURTS AND PAINS,
>
> THAT ARE BROUGHT INTO AND DEVELOP IN A MARRIAGE.
>
> JESUS PULLS DOWN ALL THE STRONGHOLDS TO PRESENT US FAULTLESS AND CLEAN.
>
> THE MEAL IS PRESENTED FULL OF GLORY.
>
> WE KNOW THAT GOD CAUSES ALL THINGS TO WORK TOGETHER FOR GOOD TO THOSE WHO LOVE GOD, TO THOSE WHO ARE CALLED ACCORDING TO HIS PURPOSE. NAS BIBLE 8:28

As I was writing this book, I paused several times because of the delicate love of a spouse: you, yours, mine and me. I also paused because of the subject matters. Yet to ignore such subject matters would be detrimental to a spouse and the marriage covenant. The truth of silence that they exist in many marriages and have damaging effects and/or affects to marriages is saddening.

There are bad ingredients and secret ingredients in marriages which need to be eliminated. A spouse or couple is suffering alone. There is a need for a sincere coach/counselor who will not only pray with a spouse or couple, but will nurture a spouse with practical assignments to perform for healing, loving and living.

A spouse needs a coach/counselor who will hold him or her accountable; Happily4Ever- After. Prayer by itself, "Ain't Gonna," fix the marriage meal. Amen.

So the dinner bell shall be rung in "Mess Hall." Why, so there can be a delicious meal served and enjoyed.. There is a spouse or couple, not to point fingers who is using the wrong ingredients, causing harm to himself, herself and marriage covenant. Plus, those close to the spouse are not using ingredients by keeping their mouth shut. The top of the box, lid of the jar or bag is closed. There are no powders, liquids, tasty, sweet, and smelling aromas escaping to fill the house. Ingredients are withheld. Nothing is coming out. No sweet aroma.

Now there are many reasons why the wrong ingredients are used and information is withheld. Look within yourself. Examine your motives. Are they right in the sight, mind and heart of God?

At the top of the marriage covenant's shopping list is a title for a recipe one desires to prepare, receive and give. It's love. Marriage is like Mash Potatoes. Get your aprons. There shall be a Happily-4Ever-After. If you said and still say "I Do" and want the marriage covenant meal, let Jesus Christ be the chef.

Pour the gravy. Taste and see that our Lord Jesus Christ is good and gracious. His desire is to withhold nothing good from us. Yes, I am a faithful Daughter of God and Wife to my husband. My husband and I have poured our gravy inside our marriage covenant. To God be all the Glory!

Contents

	Forward	vii
	From the Author	xi
Introduction	Marriage is like Mash Potatoes	xvii
Chapter 1	Correlation	1
Chapter 2	Troubled Marriages - which we can all learn from	5
Chapter 3	Maintaining Marriage: - which we can all learn from	24
Chapter 4	Coming Into Marriage: - which we can all learn from	27
Chapter 5	Peel Potatoes: - Ears, eyes, nose and mouth are placed	32
Chapter 6	Stir Me	36
Chapter 7	Boundaries	40
Chapter 8	Celibacy In Marriage	54
Chapter 9	Let Me Tell You	69
	Refreshed Ready For A Delicious Meal	71
	A Word From My Husband – I shall share	77
	Revive Us Again	79

Three Strand Cord · · · · · · · · · · · · · · · · · 81
Carol's Daughter of God
Inspirational Cards · · · · · · · · · · · · · · · · · 85
Other Books by Carol · · · · · · · · · · · · · · 87
Stay in Touch w/ Me · · · · · · · · · · · · · · · 89
Appreciation · 91
Resources · 95
References · 97
About the Author · · · · · · · · · · · · · · · · · 101

INTRODUCTION
Marriage is like Mash Potatoes

§

"MARRIAGE IS LIKE MASH POTATOES." It sure is. I remember when I was growing up as a child, in Queens, New York, I had this toy, "Mr. Potato Head." Some of you might remember the toy.

MR. POTATO HEAD FUNNY FACE KIT

WILKIPEDIA REPORTED
Mr. Potato Head" is an American toy consisting of a plastic model of a potato, which can be decorated with a variety of plastic parts that can attach to the main body. These parts usually include ears, eyes, shoes, a hat, a nose, and a mouth. The toy was invented and developed by George

Lerner in 1949, and first manufactured and distributed by Hasbro in 1952." "Over the years, the original toy was joined by "Mrs. Potato Head" and supplemented with accessories such as a car and a boat trailer. [Wikipedia, the free encyclopedia enm.wilkipedia.org]

RHEMA WORD
Mr. Potato Head was born on May 1.

Therefore, ask our Heavenly Father for advice –wise counsel.

May I have your daughter's hand in marriage; is she my wife?

May I marry this man; is he the man you choose for me?

CHAPTER 1
Correlation

§

I'LL SHARE WITH YOU WHAT our Heavenly Father shared with me. First let me say this, the title "Marriage is Like Mash Potatoes" and "Mr. Potato Head" had me laughing with intrigue.

Mr. and Mrs. Potato Head as I said earlier consist of two plastic potatoes:

> Which can be decorated with a variety of plastic parts that can attach to the main body. These parts usually include ears, eyes, shoes, a hat, a nose, and a mouth." "Over the years, the original toy was joined by Mrs. Potato Head and supplemented with accessories such as a car and a boat trailer. [Wikipedia]

Correlation! Mr. and Mrs. acquired material things years later as most married couples do; acquired together and separately. There's clothing and accessories for the man and clothing and accessories for the woman.

Correlation! God is our Creator. Oh Lord from the ground you created man and woman, two potatoes, Mr. and Mrs., husband and wife.

Dust of the ground. The potato is placed in the ground to grow and develop. Man is created from the dust of the ground and woman from the rib of the dust of the ground; the rib of man. [Genesis 2:22-24 ESV]

Man and woman are buried with Jesus Christ and rise to new life.

We were buried therefore with him by baptism into death, in order that, just as Christ was raised from the dead by the glory of the Father, we too might walk in newness of life. [Romans 6:4 ESV]

CORRELATION! RAW AND ROUGH

Man and woman are raw and rough coming into relationships. Raw does not mean you are new to relationships, but you are unaware of significant or symbolic and aggravating behavior and attitudes, components or ingredients, since we are talking about "Marriage is like Mash Potatoes," of your spouse. You nor I don't know all who and what of our spouse. We learn and re-learn in the marriage. And, to be true and obedient with the Word of God, we must ask God for our daily bread, first for our self and then for interacting with and responding to our spouse. Amen. Clear instructions are in Matthew 6:9-11.

9. Our Father in heaven, hallowed be your name,
10. Your kingdom come, your will be done on earth as it is in heaven.
11. Give us today our daily bread.

We would like to know our spouse and we will in time, but not 100 percent or totally. I'll be nice we may know 80 to 90 percent about our spouse. Initially in marriage we learn and mature. We are not cognizant of one another consciously and unconsciously. Both spouses need and require daily nourishment and cultivation. An added ingredient is counseling and/or coaching. Share the tender loving care daily.

Plants need nourishment as well, which produce in this instance a potato. A potato goes through a process to be presented in harvest time or for us to have a great harvest. A man and woman go through a process as well. I am not even talking about the spiritual mental imagery of God our creator, nor the conception and womb I am speaking about periods of childhood through adulthood and continual.

The right environment is essential for the growth and development of a potato, man and woman. What shape will develop? What thoughts and behavioral patterns will develop?

Development occurs and life continues to unfold. Early on in life before we met our spouse, events, people and circumstances happened, which helped shape us and our spouse's life.

Some of those nutrients were helpful and some were not. Some ingredients left a bad taste which can be washed away; by the water and blood of Jesus Christ and counseling. Also by your determination to mature into the person our creator created you and I to be and do.

Our childhood development had ingredients such as thoughts and behavior which laid a foundation. That foundation at times must be uprooted and re-developed for real. Childhood ears heard; eyes saw; nose smelled; and mouth spoke or stayed silent. Overall our childhood planted good seeds for mature growth.

Thank God for His son Jesus Christ's life, death and resurrection. Thank God Himself for creating man and woman from the dust of the ground.

New Life in Jesus Christ!

CHAPTER 2

Troubled Marriages - which we can all learn from

§

I CAN IMAGINE SPOUSES EXPERIENCING seasons of joy and pain. I also imagine and know how God through his Son Jesus Christ replaced pain with joy.

God is concerned about what we say and how we respond verbally and psychically to and with our spouse. God is concerned about what we hear from our spouse. What we hear is so important. Do we hear internally from our fears, hurts, past and present or do we hear our spouse's internal fears, hurts, past and present? What we hear might be one reason for the pain God can replace with healing and joy.

Are we responding to our spouse's question? Are we responding with the voice and love of God our creator?

As a paralegal, I assist in numerous criminal trials. I display exhibits electronically for the court, primarily for the prosecution team; frequently for defense. I listen very attentively to questions asked by attorneys and judge. I also listen very attentively to witnesses' responses. So many witnesses don't answer the question asked by counsel, whether the question is asked by the prosecutor or defense attorney or judge. When this occurs, I quietly say to myself, "that's not what was asked or will you please respond to the question."

There are also times when a witness is considered a "hostile witness."

A Person who (in the court's opinion) gives adverse testimony or displays hostility or prejudice against the party which called him or her to testify. [http://www.businessdictionary.com/definition/hostile-witness.html Copyright©2015 WebFinance, Inc]

"Heart and Ear"

Let the heart hear what our Lord is saying. Let the ear hear what our Lord is saying:

He heals the brokenhearted and binds up their wounds. [Psalm 147:3 ESV]

There's trouble in the field of the marriage covenant: sickness, intimacy, sex, and unemployment. Many spouses push their spouse away deliberately or subconsciously when he or she feels inadequate or emotionally disturbed. The spouse doing the pushing away knows that their spouse is in need of or desires some tenderness. Trust me, the spouse being "push away" is well aware of the emotional weather of their spouse. But now that emotional weather from the other spouse has affected the other spouse and marriage covenant. The effect on the marriage covenant is emotional turmoil. Withholding! Is this right? NO. Is it Selfish? YES. Is it Immature? YES. A spouse must ask him or herself, is my behavior pleasing to God? Am I trusting God to restore or supply? God will override your deficiency with provision and increase your ability to fulfill you and your spouse.

You and your spouse are still alive. Feel the joy and pleasure of being with one another. You are blessed. There is hope and confidence in the Jesus Christ. [Jeremiah 17: 6-8 ESV] Hear and stand on the word of our Lord. Don't be a run-way spouse. To the spouse withholding and the spouse standing, don't be a run- away spouse [unless there is abuse] God shall supply all your needs. God will show you how to make wealth; have joy and perfect peace. He will establish the works of your hands. Remember you shall not be ashamed for trusting in the Lord our God. [Psalm 40:15; 35:25; 70:3 25:3; 119:6; Isaiah 50:7 Romans 1:16-17; Joel 2:26; 1 Peter 4:16 & Isaiah 28:16]

Therefore this says the Lord God, "behold, I am laying in Zion a stone, a tested stone. A costly cornerstone for the foundation firmly placed. He who believes in it will not be disturbed [ashamed] when faced with emotional, heart burdens and dismay. [Psalm 25:20 & 31:1] Affirmed

Remember no verbal, sexual, financial or physical abuse. There are many displays of abuse that no spouse should impose nor suffer. I read an article shared by Focus on the Family (Canada) Association which a dear friend Rev. Diva aka Dr. Toni Hawkins, a self-care counsellor, posted on facebook, **Words that bruise: How to know you're in an emotionally abusive marriage.**

The article provides "practical advice and insights from marriage experts."

What exactly is emotional abuse? How do you recognize it, and what do you do if you discover you're in a destructive relationship?

"Any treatment that may diminish the sense of identity, dignity and self-worth." – Vancouver Coastal Health Authority

"Any behavior that does not affirm or nurture another's unique sense of self. Rather, it engages intentional and purposeful action to diminish a person's identity and personal power." Pauline Jewett Institute of Women's and Gender Studies, Carleton University.

While what's wrong in your relationship isn't necessarily your fault, Vernick says that a constantly humble attitude may actually be enabling your spouse to continue in their destructive patterns.

"We want to be nice because we think that's what God has called us to be," she says. "The problem is, when we aren't honest with our own human limitations and we're not honest with our own personhood, we [try to] become God for another person. When you're blind to your own enabling, that becomes dysfunctional and destructive to both of you."

What does Scripture say about you?

Does the truth about your marital health feel too much to bear? Gregory recommends diving into Scripture to see yourself in the context of Biblical truth. "You may not be able to talk to anyone about this yet," she says, "but if you look at what God says about you – 'I have called you by name, you are Mine'– it can be a huge place to begin when *who you are not* is all you have been hearing."

Start with this small sampling of Biblical truths:

> "For you created my inmost being; you knit me together in my mother's womb. I praise you because I am fearfully and wonderfully made; your works are wonderful, I know that full well." (Psalm 139:13-14) "For we are His workmanship created in Christ Jesus for good works, which God prepared beforehand, that we should walk in them." (Ephesians 2:10) "For I know the plans I have for you, declares the Lord, plans for welfare and not for evil, to give you a future and a hope." (Jeremiah 29:11)

It's scary to go to a doctor if you have a lump somewhere," Vernick says, "but if you don't pay attention and you don't know what you're dealing with, you can't get it fixed. In the same way, it's really important that we open our eyes and allow God to show us what we need to see.

The person being abused will have to ask themselves, what am I willing to live with, and what am I no longer willing to accept?" Gregory says. "If that person isn't going to make changes, you can't make changes for them, and you can't make *them* make changes. But if you make no changes, you know what it's going to be like because you're already there.

Author suggested three practical steps for moving your marriage in a different direction.

<u>Speak up.</u> Speak to your spouse with respect, but be honest and vulnerable, rather than keeping everything in and growing bitter and resentful.

1. <u>Stand up.</u> Establish boundaries in your relationship. Stay in control of the situation and draw the boundary on yourself rather than your spouse. For example, if your spouse has road rage when driving, say, "Stop driving like that, or I won't travel with you," rather than, "Can you please slow down when you're driving?"
2. <u>Step back.</u> If your spouse refuses to reach back and reconcile after you speak up and stand up for yourself, tell them that they need to respect you or that you will have to place distance between the two of you. If you feel this step is necessary but are unsure of how to proceed, please call us at 1.800.661.9800. Ask to speak with the counselling assistant who will arrange for a mutually convenient time for one of our counsellors to speak with you. [© 2013 Focus on the Family (Canada) Association]

Abuse is a negative ingredient. Sexual, financial or physical displays of abuse have effects on a spouse and marriage covenant I am a Survivor of my first marriage.

The word "Lie" is in the middle of Believe. A lie in the form of trouble always slips in some way or another. "You be and do what God has approved. "Be ye doers of the word and not hearers only, deceiving your own selves."[James 1:22]

We all lack wisdom from time to time. Ask God in any version of the bible you choose for wisdom. Trust, He has ministered to every type of personality of a spouse. God has equipped His counselors to administer therapy to you and your spouse. Remember self-care is very important.

Ladies these sisters are equipped: Rev. Dr. Toni Hawkins, Rev. Dr. Vikki Johnson, Apostle Angela Thomas and Rev. Dr. LaTonia Taylor-Bey. Men there are brothers who are equipped to minister to you as well: Tony A. Gaskins and Lamar Tyler. Couples, there are Jimmy and Karen Evans, Pastors Kenneth and Tresti and Pastors Keith and Tammy McNair and Rev. Dr. Trenace Nikki and Gregory; reach out to them on facebook.

I did not want to wait until the end of the book to list resources. Sometimes, you have to stop what you are doing and seek self-care. I did.

One evening I saw an image of a potato with sprouts while I was relaxing in my living room. I was like what? Then I got it, oh I got it. I said, "Lord I got it."

See, the Spirit of God was showing me more correlations of man, woman and a potato. I was being shown what trouble looks like and what I think when trouble appears from my husband. I have looked at my spouse as if he had sprouts sticking outside of his head and guess what? He has looked at me the same way too. We had to surrender to the head of our lives, Jesus Christ, the son of God.

Remember, Daily Bread. We had to remember the love we have for one another and God for His instructions. In Ephesians 4:15 Paul reminds us to speak the truth in love. We are to grow up in all aspects into Him who is the head, even Christ. A spouse can sing, "trouble in my way, trouble in my home and trouble all around me. "Well a potato can display the say words through sprouts. Sing or display, either way, troubles and sprouts must be cut out.

JESUS WANTS TO SAVE MARRIAGES JUST AS MUCH AS HE WANTS TO SAVE INDIVIDUALS

That image of a potato with sprouts lead me to research, goggle today, "potato sprouts." Sprouts are toxic!

RachaelRay, answered a question:

"Is it safe to eat potatoes when the eyes have sprouted? I have heard that they can be poisonous but have a hard time believing it - what's the scoop?

Thanks, Bob A.

Dear Bob:

A sprout of any size can be toxic, but you'd have to eat many sprouts to get sick. Potato *sprouts are considered* toxic due to their potentially high concentration of glycoalkaloids, which can exert their toxic effects on the nervous system by interfering with the body's ability to regulate acetylcholine, a chemical responsible for conducting nerve impulses. Phew - got that?

In addition, when potatoes sprout, the starch in the potatoes is converted into sugar. If the potato is firm, it has most of the nutrients intact and can be eaten **after removing the sprouted part**. However, if the potato is shrunken and wrinkled, it should not be eaten.

Sometimes potatoes develop a green tinge - a potato exposed to light, sprouted or un-sprouted, may itself have an increased concentration of glycoalkaloids. If this is the case, the toxic area will turn green. You can cut the green part off and eat the rest of the potato. [Rachael Ray, "Questions for the Cook – Aug 30, 2011, ©

2015 Rachael Ray Digital LLC Facebook Team Rachael or Twitter @TeamRachael] www.rachaelray. com/2011/08/is-it-safe-to-eat-sprouted-potatoes]

Here is some more information from Ask Dr. Sears:

The starch Rachael Ray reported on, "the starch in the potatoes is converted into sugar." Well according to Dr. Sears. too much sugar in the human body promotes diabetes, heart disease & obesity. [http:// www.askdrsears.com/topics/feeding- eating/familynutrition/sugar/harmful-effects-excess-sugar]

Organic Information Services Pvt Ltd posted on facebook an answer to "Potato Sprouts: Are They Good?"

Potato sprouts are certainly not healthier than normal potatoes. When potatoes sprout, the starch in the potatoes is converted into sugar. Research has suggested that if the main part of the potato is still firm, then it has most of its nutrients intact and can be eaten after removing the sprouted part. However, if the potato is shrunken and wrinkled, it should not be eaten.

What about green potatoes? Green potatoes are a result of the potato being excessively exposed to light.

After being overexposed to light, the skin becomes green due to the formation of an alkaloid called solanine which is toxic even in very small amounts. This poison is found in entire plant but the concentration is more in green potatoes and sprouts. And consumption of potatoes with green skin or sprouts of the potato plant may cause poisoning. So it is essential to remove these before eating a potato. It is always advisable to not touch or consume any unknown plant. Its important to wash hands after working in gardens. […]

How can you control potato sprouts?

Potato sprouts can be controlled using various techniques such as temperature control, moisture control, use of chemical inhibitors and use of various oils such as clove oil [...]
https://www.organicfacts.net/organic-products/organic-food/potato-sprouts-are-they-good.html
©2015 Organic Information Services

There is a field. There is a home. Both have creation within, which requires a lot of tender loving care, to produce a harvest. [© 2015 Daughter of God Inspiration Cards]

Cultivate emotional intimacy
Re-discovery your passion.
Communicate
Go on Vacation Together

Couples Vacation
Fall in love again and again and again with your spouse

I am not going to put couples who have experienced trouble in their marriage or have divorced on display by mentioning their names. Why, because I have, you have and they had hard heads like potatoes. *Correlation*

The Word of God is water to every thought and intention of the heart as irrigation is good for soil which has become dry. We shall thirst for water to live in the manner God designed for marriage [© 2015 Daughter of God Inspiration Cards]

POTATO AND MAN/WOMAN
For the word of God is living and active and sharper than any two-edged sword, and piercing as far as the division of soul and spirit, of both joints and marrow, and able to judge the thoughts and intentions of the heart. [Hebrews 4:18 ESV]

I subscribe to Unveiled Wife. Here is a facebook post:

Prayer: Don't Be Burdened By Disappointment I pray for wives like me who struggle with unmet expectations. Wives who are burdened by disappointment in marriage. I pray that You would cover our hearts and protect them from harboring negative thoughts like this. I ask Your Holy Spirit to defend us and encourage us. Help us to

extend grace to our husbands and to live joyfully no matter the circumstances. I pray for wives today and ask that You help each one of us in our marriages to thrive in Jesus' name AMEN!
[Unveiled Wife Sun, March 15, 2015]

Don't listen to what others say negatively about you. Or to what they intentionally do to, try to make you feel uncomfortable or excluded.

Look to Jesus who stirs in good ingredients. He nurtures you to grow to maturity.

Remember self-care. You must love yourself first. Stand in your confidence. Who were you before you married? What does the Word of God say about you?

I started to write look to your spouse, Nope. He or She may be the problem. Look to God where all your help comes from.

A song of ascent. I look up toward the hills. From where does my help come? [Psalm 121:1 ESV]

Lift up your eyes and look to the heavens: Who created all these? He who brings out the starry host one by one and calls forth each of them by name. Because of his great power and mighty strength, not one of them is missing. [Isaiah 40:26 ESV]

A song of ascent. I lift up my eyes to you, to you who sit enthroned in heaven. [Psalm 123:1 ESV]

Confidence in God
Comfort yourself in the Lord God

Matthew Henry wrote:

The safety of the godly. We must not rely upon men and means, instruments and second causes. Shall I depend upon the strength of the hills? upon princes and great men? No; my confidence is in God only. Or, we must lift up our eyes above the hills; we must look to God who makes all earthly things to us what they are. We must see all our help in God; from him we must expect it, in his own way and time. This psalm teaches us to comfort ourselves in the Lord, when difficulties and dangers are greatest. It is almighty wisdom that contrives, and almighty power that works the safety of those that put themselves under God's protection. He is a wakeful, watchful Keeper; he is never weary; he not only does not sleep, but he does not so much as slumber. Under this shade they may sit with delight and assurance. He is always near his people for their protection and refreshment. The right hand is the working hand; let them but turn to their duty, and they shall find God ready to give them success. He will take care that his people shall not fall. Thou shalt not be hurt, neither by the open assaults, nor by the secret attempts of thine enemies. The Lord shall prevent the evil thou fearest, and sanctify, remove, or lighten the evil thou feelest. He will preserve the soul, that it be not defiled by sin, and disturbed by affliction; he will preserve it from perishing eternally. He will keep thee in life and death; going out to thy labor in the morning of thy days, and coming home to thy rest when the evening of old age calls thee in. It is a protection for life. The Spirit, who is their Preserver and Comforter, shall abide with them forever. Let us be found in our work, assured that the blessings promised in this psalm are ours. [Matthew Henry's Concise Commentary121:1-8] Husbands, love your wives, and do not be harsh with them. [Colossians 3:19 ESV]

Listen together to, "Ain't No Stopping Us Now."
Here are a few of the lyrics:

There've been so many things that have held us down
But now it looks like things are finally comin' around, yeah
I know we've got a long long way to go, yeah
And where we'll end up
I don't know
But we won't let nothing hold us back
We gonna get ourselves together
We gonna polish up our act, yeah [McFadden & Whitehead Ain't No Stopping Us Now Released 1979]

**Upward Movement
Rising movement:
Climbing Up:**

"We must be willing to let go of the life we planned so as to have the life that is waiting for us." ~ Joseph Campbell

S o u l: A spouse has a soul. There is a **"U"** in soul. You have a responsibility to God and your spouse. Be intimate. Open up to your spouse and let God. He will provide instructions with good nutrients. God wants to enter your life. Do you want Him to order your steps in marriage? There is an abundance of growth and peace that develops when both spouses allow the Word of God to minister to their troubles. **Warning**: don't play victim or manipulate or play sick or use sickness in your marriage. I am speaking to the men especially and then the women. Women we are not here to fix men, nor are men here to fix women. Men **Don't** start "chipping away at your woman [Who women are]," as my sister Yvette would say, by asking "Why you wear lipstick or color your hair or want to work, etc." Man you stepped to her, are in a relationship with her and married to her. Cheer and celebrate your woman [women]. If she stepped to you, you are still with her. LOL.

I know and see women cheering and celebrating their man [men]. Yes, there is a man [men] who cheers and celebrates his woman [women]. I applaud you.

Some spouses have developed sores like sprouts in the marriage but God. Jesus can mend the broken hearted spouse and strengthen the marriage covenant. God though His son Jesus Christ cares so much about each and both of you. Can we sing" Lead me, Guide me Jesus?

Let the butter and gravy, symbolic in this passage, as the blood of Jesus, which can forgive, wash away, heal, restore and so much more in the marriage covenant.

> ⁴ Surely he took up our pain and bore our suffering,
> yet we considered him punished by God, stricken by him, and afflicted.
> ⁵ But he was pierced for our transgressions,
> he was crushed for our iniquities;
> the punishment that brought us peace was on him,
> and by his wounds we are healed. Isaiah 53:4-5 (NIV)

I encourage you to listen together to, "How Awesome Is Our God by Israel & New Breed, featuring Yolanda Adams." Encourage yourselves with songs.

Marriages have situations-seasons yet there is the blood of Christ. Vashawn Mitchells sings, "His blood still works it never lost its' power." You can feast on that. We have so many toppings not to cover up but to enhance the marriage covenant. Vegetables, meats and foods such as chili broccoli, cheese, bacon, chives, sour cream and steak with mushroom and onion. Dress your marriage with love.

Oh, Jesus can correct and redirect a spouse. I know it would be easy and nice if you and I could fix or decorate our spouse. But we can't. He or She is not a plastic part of toy or game Mr. and Mrs. Potato Head. Our spouses are real people, created by God with love. Each spouse has free will. When both spouses are committed to their marriage covenant and let Jesus in they can turn a bland potato into a meal and meal into a feast.

One evening I went to I-Hop to get something to eat while I waited for my mechanic to arrive at his shop. My van needed repair. As I waited for my waitress to bring my tea and turkey sandwich, I overheard two men talking. I made sure I continued to listen after I heard what they were talking about and because of who they were. Leadership, integrity and marriage were the topics on my table, but on their table, the topics were marriage infidelity, secrets, lies, poor leadership, silly women and membership.

In this field there was Crop 1: There were two married men, one pastor and one elder. The pastor was talking on his cellphone to a woman who was a member of their church. The woman informed the pastor that she was traveling to Florida. The pastor relays the information to the elder. "The elder tells the pastor to tell the woman on the cellphone that he would have helped her pay her airfare and hotel if she had told him earlier." The woman on the phone said, "Sister M is with me and Sister M said to tell you if you coming then all three of us can share the bed." Crop 2. The pastor and elder begin to talk about how their wives check their credit card statements. The Elder said, "that's why I always use cash."

Discipline is not to destroy. Discipline is to respect the marriage covenant. I am going to go plant another seed. Discipline is to respect your brother and sister's covenant. It's not good to cause harm or destroy a spouse with toxic chemicals and unhealthy nourishments from another spouse, male or female.

Krishann Briscoe has a blog to encourage couples and divorcee that are going through hard times. Check her out on facebook and twitter.

I also subscribe to Together 4 Ever. Isaac Kubvoruno posted: God said the two shall be one. Fight to keep other people out of your marriage. Therefore what God has joined together let no mother, sister, or family put asunder. [Together4Ever: Facebook: Facebook. com/4keeps; Twitter:

CHAPTER 3
Maintaining Marriage: - which we can all learn from

§

ONE DAY THE SPIRIT OF God said, "Some people see my Glory but don't seem." I asked God, "How can they see your glory and not see you"? He said, "They see want and not serve." Some people are trying to control God. Who's controlling who? God, Jesus and Holy Spirit are in control. Get your heart and mind nourished with the Word of God. Serve. Our dear 4 ever with us sister, Whitney Houston, who is singing in the heavenly choir, reminds us in her song there's "Somebody Bigger than You and I."

There is a difference in want and serve. Our Father said. "Some people see want and they manipulate, instigate, dominate, steal, rob and kill; when people serve they see God who gives freely; there is no need to manipulate, instigate, dominate steal, rob and kill. A person who serves God and has a relationship with Him, God gives wealth, health and prosperity.

Are you cultivating or destroying God's covenant marriage? Are you allowing others and things to take priority in your marriage? Serve one another directly and indirectly.

Be very sure to respect one another's gifts and callings in God's worship houses, home, corporations or entrepreneurships. Serving God goes beyond the marriage and altar. Make time for vacations and cuddling Leave love notes; plant them around the house, lunch bag, coat pocket, in your spouse's car. You get the idea.

Now that both spouses have said I do 4Evermore to each other and God, keep God in your marriage covenant. The Word of God ministers to each spouse individually as well as together for unity. Are you cultivating or destroying God's covenant marriage?

Prep yourself before you enter the field of marriage and throughout the marriage with the Word of God, which is nourishment 4Evermore. You won't be rare or raw in every situation or incident. You will learn to forgive, endure, ignore and have patience. In addition, you will learn to continue to pursue God's plans for you unencumbered. Remember, the Word of God is always your foundation.

One Potato Two Potato not three Potato Four
As newborn babes, desire the sincere milk of Word, that you may grow thereby. [1 Peter 2;2 KJV]

Proper Nutrients: Fertilization
Tender care is required for a potato, man and woman. Nothing short of the Glory of God. Fertilization is important.

Fertilization: Developing healthy plants necessary for maximum tuber growth requires that all essential nutrients be supplied at optimal rates. Both deficit and excess fertilizer situation can reduce tuber bulking rates. Nutrient deficiencies limit canopy growth and shorten canopy duration resulting in reduced carbohydrate production and tuber growth rates. Excessive fertilizer applications can cause nutrient imbalances that delay or slow tuber growth rates. [Robert B. Dwelle and Stephen L. Love, http://www.babble.com/relationships/25-quotes-to-encourage- you-during-tough-times-in-your-marriage]

CHAPTER 4
Coming Into Marriage: - which we can all learn from

§

CHILDHOOD IDEOLOGY IS PEELED AWAY as with the skin of a potato. Who, what and where of past and present instances or circumstances which is not pleasing to God must be washed away. Why? Because the marriage will face uninvited trouble! Everyone has not matured. Childhood ideology must be peeled away.

Now some people, places, and things who and which surrounded Mr. and Mrs. Potato Head from the past and present must not dominate, manipulate or regulate the Will of God in the covenant marriage. Oh this includes family, children, friends, job, sports, media, organizations, including religious organization.

There is an "US" is husband; husband and wife come together. US: not I or them.

Jesus takes away the sins of the world. Childhood, young -adult and world-wide sin is destroyed or replaced with new life. There are behavioral modifications in a spouse. A spouse who has been nurtured by the Word of

God and planted in the Kingdom of God will hear, smell and talk differently. A spouse in the Kingdom of God, which is good, will display the image of Jesus Christ.

Remember temptations will come. However, you can overcome temptation.

No temptation has overtaken you that is not common to man God is faithful, and he will not let you be tempted beyond your ability, but with the temptation he will also provide the way of escape, that you may be able to endure it. 1 Corinthians 10:13 ESV]

Temptation is symbolic to insects that enter a garden of potatoes or appear at your outdoor and inside activity. There are harmless pesticides to eliminate temptations.

Before you were raw, hard and bland, but Thanks Be to God!

The Bible states that in the very beginning of the human race God created man in His own image, in the image of God He created him; male and female He created them. God blessed them and said to them, "Be fruitful and increase in number; fill the earth and subdue it." [Genesis 1:27-28] In other words, the Biblical record is clear: God created men and women equal, Period. Dominion over everything was given to the woman as well as to the man. The woman was not created inferior to the man; nor was the man greater than the woman. [Written by Anne Graham Lotz]

Jesus Christ is the head of each spouse. Each spouse should have the mind of Christ. Are there basic roles for a spouse; Yes. Do roles shift for a season; Yes. Communicate honestly with one another and respect one's view. [Philippians 2:5; 1Cor.2:16b.] God is husband. [Isaiah 54:5 ESV]

There is a development in one's sight with Jesus Christ. There is discernment, understanding, communication and aroma. God will, if you receive, as the ground receives seed, change your outlook of you and your spouse.

Water is essential for marriage. Sometimes there is boiling water to remove impurities or cold water to cool off or warm water to soak and relax. Your marriage needs water like a potato. Water will generate a change.

A spouse or couple should remember that you or they were not created by God or united to enjoy yourself only; but you were created by God for a purpose. Married couples are on display for others to see the great works of Jesus. [Matthew 5:16 ESV]. Stop showing out, stop the tantrums and start showing God's Glory.

Your ears, eye, noise, mouth, hands, feet and acquired material things because of God. Here are a few reminders in 1 Peter 5:6, Psalm 16:2 Psalm 73:25, Isaiah 44:5 and John 15:5 Created for His Glory. [Isaiah 43:7 ESV]

God's Covenant Marriage. [Gen 2:21-2 4ESV] Allow God to impart and improve what's needed. Don't quench the work of the Holy Spirit.

God created marriage no government or subcommittee envisioned it. No social organization developed

it. Marriage was conceived and born in the mind of God. [Max Lucado]

Remember Jesus Christ is the head of Mr. Potato and Mrs. Potato. In our reality His ways are perfect. His way is truth and life. WOW just saying "The Breath of God" makes me feel wonderful. The Breath of God reminds me of a well done steak and baked potato. The Word of God is milk and meat, nourishment, to the bones; salt to our life and style in this world.

The husband and wife most definitely have different shapes, but both are wonderfully and fearfully made. Think about the different shapes and colors of potatoes. Potatoes are served in various forms: fried, baked, sliced, creamy, cold or hot with numerous toppings. Tasty.

A husband and wife after God's own heart hear and feel the "Art of Love. If you are single preparing for marriage and your special someone won't change, you can't change him or her nor save him or her. Remove yourself from harm's way, free your mind; they may never choose to be free.

I preached a sermon on Good Friday. The 4th word from the cross, *"My God, my God, why have you forsaken me?" [Matthew 27:46 and Mark 15:34] My sermon topic was* "THE FLOOR OF THE CROSS." The floor of the cross is a reminder, for us and communities world-wide, from house to house to RELEASE all rotten, perceptions, personalities, positions, persons, problems and plans not of Jesus to the floor of the cross. Well, since I'm in the marriage field, one must drop all their single mess at the floor of the cross to enter into a covenant marriage. If Miss or Mr. has a problem respecting being in committed relationship, then you should not have a problem putting the trash out. Are you praying with me? Are you praying for yourself and marriage? Please do Jesus prayed in the 9th hour; repeat "9th hour," for us, on the cross."

God wants all sin bagged, tied up and deposited in the grave.

Someone is married or in a committed relationship masquerading as "Walking Solo" when you're in a committed relationship. Place that "Walking Solo" at the floor of the cross.

One Potato Two Potato not three Potato Four

CHAPTER 5

Peel Potatoes: - Ears, eyes, nose and mouth are placed

§

In Chapter 4 I mentioned that I preached a sermon on Good Friday, "The Floor of the Cross.' Well, the floor of the cross is also a reminder for spouses world- wide from house to house to RELEASE all rotten, perceptions, personalities, positions, problems and plans not of Jesus, to the floor of the cross. "Bring it on down," place it at THE FLOOR OF THE CROSS." THE FLOOR OF THE CROSS – THE GRAVE 6 feet under where TRANSITION TO TRANSFOR-MATION continues. Transition is the result of prayer. Are your praying? Are you praying the right prayers?

PRAY
Prepare your **R**esponse to **A**lign **Y**ielding to Jesus Christ.
I ask the same question, I asked in Chapter 4. Are you praying with me? Are you praying for yourself and marriage? Please do. Jesus prayed in the 9th hour; repeat, "9th hour," for us, on the cross."

Lay it all down ON THE FLOOR OF THE CROSS. There are marriages wherein a wife is calling herself "Ms." or "Miss" instead of Mrs. She is creating a MESS for herself, spouse and children. She don't even know who her baby daddy is. Don't forget your families and communities. Lest not forget your life and the life of the one you are creeping with sleeping with, lying too, the one on the other side of town.

There is a husband calling himself the man and not husband. He is creating a MESS. Baby over here; baby over there; You too are creating a MESS. for yourself, spouse and children. Don't forget your families and communities. Lest not forget your life and the life of the one you creeping with, sleeping with, lying too, the one on the other side of town.

One night I was having a conversation with my daughter about one of her girlfriends. I said, "she needs a relationship with Jesus." My daughter said, "MA, she goes to church." I looked at her and started laughing then got serious again. I said what the Holy Spirit told me. "Some people say they go to church to worship and hear from God, but their body is there only. Their mind is on the other side of town." Remember the O'Jays song, "<u>Your Body is Here With Me (But Your Mind's On The Other Side Of Town)</u>?" Well, that's the way it is for some individual and spouse who are cheating. Stop messing God around with your secret relationships, thoughts and behavior. Do you think you are hidden? As a dear friend Schylon would say, "That's a Hot Mess."

You send cards and gifts to family, especially friends who are known by both of you, introduced to you by your spouse, with your name only. Not your name with your spouse's name or Mr. and Mrs.; but your name ONLY. What are you doing? You are creating a mess: distrust, confusion, chaos and lack of respect. Sign the card the proper way. [We are not referring to specialty cards such as to dad, mom, daughter, niece brother or sister; then if we are, send one with your name and with both your name with your spouse]

PRAYER
Jesus your name has all power and authority. Remove all the rotten, stiff-neck, jealous, lusting and out of order from your marriage covenant. Oh Lord, only your ingredients. Peel the skin of selfishness, self- centeredness. Peel the rottenness of harbored feelings. Purify the hearts and minds of everyone that is married or desire to enter into your marriage covenant. Do whatever you need to do Jesus to heal marriages; even the thought of marriage.
Lord your precious children, who were born from a love or lust relationship outside of the marriage covenant of Mr. and Mrs., wrap your loving arms around the children. Let the children know that they are loved. That you will provide for them. That you will minister to their parents and the spouse of their mother or father. Release your love. Children belong to you Oh God. Lord, I ask that you minister to all. Be their God, order their steps. Pour your love and resources to and through them for the children; for their marriage I pray you stir up the gifts in your children. I pray for forgiveness for the parents. I pray for the brokenhearted spouse; I pray that everyone will be as I say "professionally polite" and in the image of Jesus Christ. In Jesus Christ name Amen.

YOU ARE PRECIOUS
© 2015 Daughter of God Inspiration Cards

© 2015 Daughter of God Inspiration Cards

CHAPTER 6
Stir Me

§

WE HAVE TWO POTATOES, TWO individuals, two spouses. I can image when God stirs gratitude on one spouse how that gratitude gets stirred back onto the other spouse. God through His son Jesus Christ stirs appreciation, complements, compassions, understanding and helping hands on one spouse to the other. Mixing and Stirring. Jesus is mixing and transferring from God to each spouse.

Then there are time as in preparing any meal that there occurs a lack of an ingredient or an ingredient gets stuck in the tube, jar or on paper. The Holy Spirit is welcomed just as water is on a hot humid day. Why, because of life's circumstances, a spouse gets stuck; a squeeze or push must occur to release the ingredient. Once the ingredient is added there is still a little more work to do. So with mash potatoes, we pull out the mixer and mix slow, medium, or fast, "Stir It real Good." Lumps are gone. [Stiff- necked –"You stiff-necked people! Your hearts and ears are still uncircumcised. You are just like your ancestors: You always resist the Holy Spirit! Acts 7:51

Now, Ingredients are blended. YUMMY

I remember as a child hearing the word, "mine," especially among married couples. I saw and heard a person in the marriage covenant refer to material acquired for the marriage as "mine." Even in my own marriage the word "mine" has been spoken.

One day the Spirit of God said, "Everything comes from me." "Share and give." [1Chronicles 29:14 ESV]

Give and it will be given to you. A good measure, pressed down, shaken together and running over, will be poured into your lap. For with the measure you use, it will be measured to you. [Isaiah 6:38 ESV]

Peel away your thoughts of it's yours alone; it belongs to God who freely gives and takes away. "Naked I came from my mother's womb, naked I'll return to the womb of the earth. Do you give to your spouse as Christ gives to the church? Stir.

Many spouses give and do more for their children and others than they do for and to their spouse. Peel and Stir.

How often do you communicate or spend time with your spouse? What plans have you made for or with your spouse? I'm just asking.

Don't let the Irrigation system or blender breakdown in your marriage covenant.

Jesus is the potter and we are the clay; mold me shape me Lord. Yes you, LORD, are our Father. We are the clay, you are the potter; we are all the work of your hand. [Isaiah 64:8 OMG, as I write, the Spirit of God is saying, "as I smash the clay I am stirring and reforming." The Potter's work with clay is very similar to mashing potatoes.

The Master's Mix

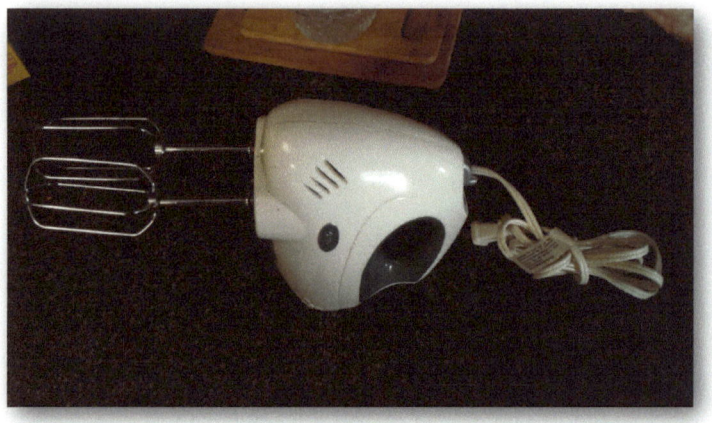

I can imagine one potato getting mashed more or one side of the bowl being blended more. Sometimes you have a stubborn or stiff-necked spouse or you have two spouses holding hands or sitting next to one another yet still harboring negative feeling. So what happens? Mash, stir and pray. Eventually the entire bowl is full of smooth creamy mash potatoes. Mash to Maturity. Stir Me. Plate Please.

Keep maturing in the Lord Jesus Christ. Let Him smooth things out in you When your spouse acts contrary to the Word of God you keep maturing and God shall keep you smooth and cool.

Do you want a good delicious meal? Well here it is, plain and simple. IT IS GOD'S ULTIMATE DESIRE TO GIVE YOU THE KINGDOM, IT IS HIS PLEAURE. [LUKE 12:32 ESV]

Knowing God's plans will strengthen you. His grace is sufficient for you to overcome and deal with smooth or hardness. Good times and bad times; throughout any weather. Don't worry; the ground will be titled again for new crop. Remember the parable of the sower in Matthew 13:10 – 23, the Word of God fell on different grounds. The Word of God is your strength. "My grace is sufficient for you, for my power is made perfect in weakness. [2 Corinthians 12:9ESV]

Withholding something of worth, value and essential from your spouse, intimacy, vacations, sex, money, acknowledgement, just to name a few, can be devastating on you marriage.

Imagine preparing a meal and omitting an essential ingredient. Curry paste or chili or garlic sauce or Cajun seasoning or coconut milk, or eggs or cinnamon or nutmeg or lemon. Omitting an essential ingredient can destroy a whole meal. Sometimes a meal can be salvaged, but most of the time that meals is trashed. It's better to have all ingredients before preparing the meal. Prepare, study and apply.

CHAPTER 7
Boundaries

§

Therefore a man shall leave his father and mother and hold fast to his wife, and the two shall become one flesh. [Ephesians 5:31 ESV]

LOVES, RESPECT AND BOUNDARIES SHALL abide. Let me say this. I am a mother, sister and friend to my daughter and sibling. I also hold affectionate titles to other family members. Boundaries I do respect. You should too.

Potatoes grow in patches, but get separated. They are individually picked and put in a bag together, but each one gets pealed or sliced. Correlation a spouse is born into a family. Later on in life, a spouse gets married and gives birth to children and there are extended families.

"MESS HALL"
Have you ever had to whisper to a relative or friend, "He or She has a spouse?" Telling a stranger is understandable or expected, but to tell a relative; Come on now! Or have you witnessed the behavior or heard comments by a relative or

friend to someone's spouse, which his or her spouse should and definitely could address, receive and give? Come on now! Sometimes it's not the innocent bystander or friend or trick misbehaving, it's the spouse; but that's another field which I might discuss in this book. So many insects enter the garden. One book can't cover them all.

For the innocent bystander or trick in the church or street: He or She is MARRIED! ~Hear me "Married."

NOW, when you have to say, "He or She has a spouse," to a relative or friend, who knows, **it's annoying,** exasperating, and frustrating. Mother! Dad! Sister! Brother! Son! Daughter! Auntie! Uncle! Cousin! Friend! You get the point. No need to go on.

Now before I continue, there is no **Obscenity or Abuse** involved in any of the relationships. The siblings, children, relatives are close. Boundaries haven't been set that's all. Communicate the boundaries then implement them.

Sometimes the relative or friend should give wise counsel ~ open their mouth to their relative or friend who's married. Son! Daughter! Brother! Sister! Mother! Etc. "You are talking, hanging out, and buying for me like I'm your spouse; TURN YOUR ATTENTION toward your SPOUSE Stop calling and coming over every day"

Here is a situation a friend told me about:

Her brother is married. He called his sister to ask her to partner with him on a treadmill. My friend told her brother, "You are married; ask your wife." Her brother and his wife have a good relationship and good credit. He was used to doing everything with his sister before he got married. New boundaries, that's all. I applaud the sister for saying wise counsel.

A spouse should communicate to their relative or sibling that his or her love for that sibling or relative will always exist.
Communicate to your relatives that you will still get together with them, just not that often. Also stop talking about your family so much to your spouse. There is so much more to talk about with your spouse other than your siblings or children. A male co-worker told me that when a man who talks about his mother or children all the time is not interested in a real relationship with a woman or he will never put his wife first. Another female co-worker told me that her fiancé always says he has to do or give this to or for his mother; therefore he has little money or time for her. I am hearing more stories about men and women who have <u>not</u> set boundaries nor have proper priorities; these people are married.

Red flags are up before marriage and trouble in marriages. Red flags can't be ignored. Boundaries are essential ingredients for creamy smooth pleasurable marriage covenant.
Parents and children will always be loved. However there is an order in the marriage covenant. This goes for Daddy girls also.
Putting your spouse first does not mean that you nor he or she loves your parents or children any less. Your spouse

comes first. Remember the word, "effect," well your marriage or upcoming marriage will be in another field that you don't want. Your spouse is interested in the children you have together and the children you had prior to the marriage. Your spouse is concerned about your parents and family. Remember you and your spouse have a life independent of others. Leave the field you were created in. You can visit from time to time. you will appreciate visiting your family more. Your spouse comes first. Leave and cleave.

Trust me your sibling (s) or relative (s) conversation with their spouse is NOT saturated with your name. Nor are you a stimulus for their interaction with one another or social events. You are affecting your marriage covenant. Your spouse is trying to have a conversation with you and all you are talking to him or her about are the children, your children or relatives. Please!

Momma and Daddy had or have their relationship or marriage. Children will grow up and have their significant other or spouse. And they sure ain't going to let you interrupt their happy home or take priority over their relationship. They have boundaries and priorities. So should you. Leave and cleave to your spouse. I laugh when I watch "Who Loves Raymond." "Oh and what about, "Monster-in-Law," with Jennifer Lopez.

Remember, earlier I told you I travel a lot for my job and personally. Well, I'll a start a conversation with almost anyone. Here is another delicate truth which is affecting marriages; I thought I was alone. NOT ALONE and neither are you. The issue involves a parent and child relationship which is taking priority over the spouse or significant other. Again, there is no Obscenity or Abuse involved nor sickness involved.. Before you ask, YES I as well as other spouses love children. Most of us were parents before we entered the marriage covenant. There are some marriages wherein this is their first child together or ever. In any event, the question is "Who is getting the attention and respect?"

I recall in past relationships and present marriage, screaming outside the presence of anyone and in a sacred place, "Who are you in bed with?" "You got your d_ _k so far up their ass and vagina." "You would think you are married to them." "Who are you making love too? Who are you f__king, Me, your mother or children?" Yeah, I was ANGRY; I had had enough!

What do you do? Start the meal over. Put all the ingredients on the table softly not slamming them hard and loud on the table. Calm down. Turn the heat down. Run cool water. Explain what you see happening. Express how you feel emotionally. Express how the behavior is affecting you and the marriage. Express what you expect. Communicate what you believe the effect will be on all parties involved and marriage covenant.

Sometimes there is no immediate change for years.. True. So what do you do? There are many options without stress or replanting [divorce]. I think many arguments occur because one spouse is shocked by the behavior or has kept quiet for so long. If you have kept quiet speak up. Seek counseling, pray and focus on you. Be angry but don't sin. Forgive. If the situation is insufferable or abusive, a spouse for their own self-care needs to leave for a season. The season will vary.

Here are a few ways I nurture me and what I implement in my marriage when the soil of my marriage gets drench. Let me say this, there is no abuse in any form. Is there turbulence? Yes. Thank God the turbulence is far less than many. I'm not shocked by unfamiliar spirits now. and matured spiritually. I know what to do. Cast down every imagination. Focus on my dreams and purpose and speak up. [trying not to hurt someone's feeling while you are hurting is not self-care] Sometimes, I leave for a season. Sometimes, I pretend that I am window shopping. 'll see the behavior or hear the conversation and pause. I'll close my eyes, breathe, and say a quick prayer. Don't buy or say it.

"I know I don't need to _____;
Lord, I love me. Lord I Love my husband;
I have to remove myself from this situation or nope, I am not attending;
Carol, breathe, pray and walk.
Lord please peel what needs to be peeled away and give me peace!

Sometimes you have to talk to yourself and your heavenly father in 3-way LOL.

I know my spouse has his way of dealing with turbulence as well. Every spouse needs a positive meal or plan. Didn't the Lord say he would make a way of escape? [Isaiah 43:6, Exodus 14:22, Psalm 77:19 ESV]

I told you in the previous chapters that the bell was going to ring in the Mess Hall. I'm trying to prepare a delicious meal.

I am respectful and honor boundaries and priorities!

I was out in what I call the Movie field seeking a movie to rent from Redbox one weekend. I rented:

> *The Dempsey Sisters*, which follows a family's dramatic pursuit of a musical dream, and stars Cymphonique Miller, Denyce Lawton, Teairra Mari, MC Lyte, Valarie Pettiford, Antwon Tanner, Lynn Whitfield, Clifton Powell, Taj En'Phiniti and Dom Santana; Produced by Eric Tomosunas. The Dempsey Sisters performed together as a singing group when they were kids, but disbanded when a record deal never materialized. The sisters come together to revise their dream with the assistance of their big brother, Thad (Antwon Tanner), a charming, fit 29-year old, who brings home his new wife, Ava (TAJ En'Phiniti), who has some surprising talents.[http://www.UPtv.com/TheDempseySisters. Facebook Shared November 2, 2014]

There's more to the story, but I want to focus on a scene involving boundaries and discuss the root of the problem. A solution is provided.

The middle sister Sheena confronts the older sister, Deena, about her attitude and behavior towards their brother's new wife, Ava. Sheena identified the problem and why it existed. She provided a solution to keep everyone in peace and harmony.

Deena was jealous of the wife. Deena wanted her brother all to herself. Deena saw herself as the favorite sister of the brother. Deena was self-absorbed. She thought she was losing her only and big brother's love, plus her best friend. Deena was in denial about her feelings at first. Towards the end of the movie Deena acknowledged her attitude and behavior was inappropriate. Deena started working on correcting her feelings and relationship towards her big brother's new wife. Deena also began to work on issues in her personal life.

The middle sister Sheena not only confronts her older sister, she informs their brother in the presence of the older sister, Deena, and younger sister, Tina, who also acknowledged and confirmed what the middle sister was discussing.
.[http://www.UPtv.com/TheDempseySisters. Facebook Shared November 2, 2014]

Now, there are tines wherein it's the spouse who feels he or she is losing or missing the sibling or parent's love and has not set proper boundaries nor set priorities. I thought I'll mention that. You know how seeds blow into the garden. That thought has actuality blown in.

There's another movie with a story line, Not Easily Broken, staring Morris Chestnut as Dave the husband and Taraji P. Henson as Clarice the wife.

Storylines

Dave and Clarice, a married couple with shards of friction working at their bonds. Their lives are instantly relatable, as they deal with waves of boredom, distraction, conflicting goals, and deep love they may sometimes take for granted. "After Clarice is injured, her overbearing mom (Jenifer Lewis) moves in to help care for her, and a chain of tests and challenges begins to unfold. The career-focused Clarice has a mini- showdown with her well intentioned mother: "In all your lessons about how to be strong, you left out some very important things," Clarice cries to her mother, (Jenifer Lewis), who snaps, "What?" [How to *love*, Mama! [*A.T. Hurley*]

Clarice has grown up in a home where the mother ruled everyone, including her ex-husband, with an iron fist. With her mother using bitterness, resentment and anger to…"
After years of disagreeing on what true happiness, success, and love really are, Dave and Clarice Johnson have finally reached a breaking point in their marriage. When Clarice is hurt in a car accident, the obvious truth that more than just her injuries need immediate attention is exposed. Their odds of making it worsen as Clarice begins to see a physical therapist, and Dave develops a friendship with Julie and her teenage son Bryson. The acceptance and

comfort he finds in them stirs his longing for a family and a passionate partner. As temptation tugs at Dave and Clarice pulls farther away, they must confront whether their vows are or are NOT EASILY BROKEN. *Written by <u>Anonymous</u>*

Clarice's mother—who wants Dave out of her daughter's life and tells him that Clarice is "more a man than you'll ever be," really just wants to protect her daughter. Her own husband hit her and walked out on her, and she wants to spare Clarice the same fate. When Clarice tells her mother that she never taught her "how to really care about someone, how to forgive," her mom says, "I gave you everything in me that he (meaning her former husband) didn't take. [Written by Anonymous]

Jump forward ten years or so and Dave and Clarice have even more to contend with. A shopping list of issues includes his dedication to a Little League Team, her dedication to her job, his desire for children, her lack of interest in those children, an impressive on- screen car accident that leaves Clarice seriously injured, and Dave's eventual attraction to Clarice's physical therapist, who has a lot of the things Dave was hoping life would give him, including a son. It's easy to see how a marriage could sever apart rapidly, but early on the couple is assured by their minister that a relationship that has man, woman, and God in it is "not easily broken." Unfortunately for Dave and Clarice, they seem to listen to Clarice's mom for guidance more frequently than God. [Reviewed By: Rafe Telsch Cinemablend]

There's a lot going on in this movie, but I want to focus on the mother, "Mary, Mama Clark, Jenifer Lewis." This movie is screaming "Boundaries Mama Clark." There is a solution. A man and woman must leave their mother and father and cleave to their spouse. Wife respect your husband in the presence of anyone; husband do likewise. Spouse stand together with your spouse. Require everyone to respect your spouse; everyone shall respect your union.

End of story, "Clarice releases herself from her controlling mother's grip so that she can make peace with her husband." [Reviewed By: Rafe Telsch Cinemablend]

BOUNDARIES
Marriages are in the Field of the Kingdom of God. Respect the union of husband and wife. God is in control not your mother, father, children siblings, friends, associates, strangers or religious officials.

Your past or present affiliates shall not dominate, manipulate or regulate the will of God in the covenant of marriage.

[http://www.wi ngclips.com/ movie-clips/not- easily broken/how-to love: http://www/en.wikipedia.org/wiki/Not_ Easily Broken

Somebody must say something in love. Stop the cycle of misunderstanding, hurt and disrespects. "Whoever has ears, let them hear" "Anyone with ears to hear should listen and understand." [Matthew 11:15 ESV]

Remember those potato sprouts? Well here are more sprouts, yelling, cussing and threatening. Stop harmful words There is one whose rash words are like sword thrusts, but the tongue of the wise brings healing. [Proverbs 12:18 ESV]

Matthew Henry - effects of the tongue:

The tongue is death or life, poison or medicine, as it is used. 1. There are words that are cutting and killing, that are *like the piercings of a sword*. Opprobrious words grieve the spirits of those to whom they are spoken, and cut them to the heart. Slanders, like a sword, wound the reputation of those of whom they are uttered, and perhaps incurably. Whisperings and evil surmises, like a sword, divide and cut asunder the bounds of love and friendship, and separate those that have been dearest to each other. 2. There are words that are curing and healing: *The tongue of the wise is health*, closing up those wounds which the backbiting tongue had given, making all whole again, restoring peace, and accommodating matters in variance and persuading to reconciliation. Wisdom will find out proper remedies against the mischiefs that are made by detraction and evil-speaking. Matthew Henry's Commentary

Your tone and words should be soft spoken in Love. Your words should be helpful; not hurtful with intent to harm. Speak the truth.

Here are some ingredients

Likewise, husbands, live with your wives in an understanding way, showing honor to the woman as the weaker vessel, since they are heirs with you of the grace of life, so that your prayers may not be hindered. Finally, all of you, have unity of mind, sympathy, brotherly love, a tender heart, and a humble mind. Do not repay evil for evil or reviling for reviling, but on the contrary, bless, for to this you were called, that you may obtain a blessing. For "Whoever desires to love life and see good days, let him keep his tongue from evil and his lips from speaking deceit; let him turn away from evil and do good; let him seek peace and pursue it. [1 Peter 3:7-12 ESV]

Let no corrupting talk come out of your mouths, but only such as is good for building up, as fits the occasion, that it may give grace to those who hear. [Ephesians 4:29 ESV]

A gentle tongue is a tree of life, but perverseness in it breaks the spirit. [Proverbs 15:4 ESV]

Keep your tongue from evil and your lips from speaking deceit.[Psalm 34:13 ESV]

We try, but we are not perfect, therefore ask God: Create in me a clean heart, O God, and renew a right spirit within me. [Psalm 51:10 ESV]

[N]ow you must put them all away: anger, wrath, malice slander, and obscene talk from your mouth.

Do not lie to one another, seeing that you have put off the old self with its practices and have put on the new self, which is being renewed in knowledge after the image of its creator. [Colossians 3:8-10 ESV]

Repay no one evil for evil, but give thought to do what is honorable in the sight of all. If possible, so far as it depends on you, live peaceably with all. [Romans 12:17-18]

Remember to Forgive

For if you forgive others their trespasses, your heavenly Father will also forgive you. [Matthew 6:14 ESV]

In the beginning, God created the heavens and the earth. The earth was without form and void, and darkness was over the face of the deep. And the Spirit of God was hovering over the face of the waters. And God said, "Let there be light," and there was light. And God saw that the light was good. And God separated the light from the darkness. God called the light Day, and the darkness he called Night. And there was evening and there was morning, the first day. [Genesis 1:1-9:29 ESV]

CHAPTER 8

Celibacy In Marriage

§

Here is Trouble and Truth.
Because you cannot perform sexually the way you did in your younger days
Because you are sick;
Because you are angry;
Because you are mourning;
Because you are not experienced;
Because you temporarily live in different States; Because your house is full of other people;
Because you choose to stay home;
Because your mommy or daddy said a particular Sex Act is wrong;
Because your pastor [male or female] said a particular Sex Act is; X-rated and prohibited;
    Because _____
        [You fill in the blank]

CELIBACY CAUSES PROBLEMS
Because is an excuse. Because is an effect and affect that needs to exit or be extracted. Negative thoughts and words leave a foul smell. Imagine a burned or rotten potato.
    You are a Son of God and Daughter of God. You have been created and changed.

Now concerning the matters about which you wrote: "It is good for a man not to have sexual relations with a woman." But because of the temptation to sexual immorality, each man should have his own wife and each woman her own husband. The husband should give to his wife her conjugal rights, and likewise the wife to her husband. For the wife does not have authority over her own body but the husband does.

Likewise the husband does not have authority over his own body, but the wife does. Do not deprive one another, except perhaps by agreement for a limited time, that you may devote yourselves to prayer; but then come together again, so that Satan may not tempt you because of your lack of self-control. [1 Corinthians 7:1-40 ESV]

    There are numerous songs about intimacy and sex.
    A Otis Redding "Try A Little Tenderness"
    B Marvin Gaye "Let's Get it on"

C R&B 90's Old School Slow Jams Pt. 4 (R&B Throwback Old School Mix) by Daddio ~Youtube
D. SOUL and R&B LOVE SONGS MIX 1990 TO 2015 ~ R. Kelly, Chris Brown, Mariah Carey, Ne-Yo, Trey Songz by Xclusive Music ~Youtube

We have seen older men marry younger women. We have seen older women marry younger men. Whatever field you find yourself in the Word of God is good for the soul. There are marriage counselors who discuss every issue of marriage including sex and intimacy.
Connect the mind, heart and body. Intimacy is not sex and sex is not intimacy, but they are both needed. Intimacy and sex make a wonderful meal. In short, getting to know-intimacy and move your body-sex.
Communicate with your spouse and embrace fresh ingredients to add to your sexual meal. In college, I used to dislike prerequisite courses, but now I appreciate prerequisite courses. Prerequisite courses provide an opportunity to communicate, explore and share thoughts. Before and in marriage there is a prerequisite called intimacy. Move pride, shy or stubbornness out of the way.
A spouse may be incapacitated but he or she is not dead. Desire is still in your mind and in the mind of your spouse. I know there are false beliefs from childhood, parents and religious man-made rules which are hindering you from receiving delicious sexual recipes and enjoying healthy sexual meals. Wash those hindrances off. There are sexual enhancements, medication, sex toys, garments role play,

bubble bath, couple or individual massages, movies, flowers, love notes, desserts severed differently. Get out of the bed and shower field. You have been there too long. There are other venues. When was the last time you returned to the ground where you died to old ways & things? Died, Buried and Resurrected. Old thing are passed away. New Life created ~ the Ground. There is sexual maturity Don't let the wind and dirt impair vision. When a spouse allows the Spirit of God to mash their negative thoughts and behavior or false beliefs from whoever, whatever and whenever there shall be a delicious healthy recipes for marriage meals.

There have been seasons since my marriage wherein celibacy and no personal intimacy [P.I], existed. My husband and I were both at fault and immature. Celibacy and no P I. are closed cells which must be opened for many reasons such as health, depression and infidelity. Celibacy and no P.I. are harmful to a spouse. Oh Me Oh My.

There were seasons wherein I felt single while I was married. However, I did not venture outside nor did my spouse venture outside our marriage covenant complicating the meal further; for those who did, you know what I am talking about. I have friends and family who have and I love them anyway. I hear their stories.

I took a step and sought counseling which saved my life and marriage; saved the woman and wife.

During my single days before marriage and before a relationship with Jesus Christ I was in a few intimate, romantic and sexually relationships. Entering into a relationship with Jesus Christ the sexual relationships ceased.

However, my desire for a sexual relationship never dissipated. I thought marriage was a ticket for me to have a delicious sexual meal to savory for life until my husband got sick. So emotionally and psychically I was a devastated when the meal was not served. Oh when the meal was served we both felt like licking the plate and folk.

Oh my husband was in his feelings as I. I was feeling angry. He was feeling not man enough. We both were feeling the other, yet no sexual healing.

Was I in love with my spouse and was he in love with me YES and YES. Were we committed to our marriage covenant? YES. However Jesus had to mash us and we added some ingredients such as patience, communication, forgiveness, individual counseling and, perseverance with much prayer.

My spouse developed cancer in the first year of our marriage and in the seventh year suffered several mini strokes, but GOD survived. Illness compounded with other issues can be overwhelming.

I was speaking with a co-worker recently who informed me that her male cousin was dying. He had stage 4 cancer. He was angry not about the cancer but about his wife. His younger wife of two years stopped coming home every night. When his wife did come home she would come in very late. Oh he was angry and was going to change his life insurance and other financial matters. He began to focus so much on his wife's behavior and responded negatively.

This spouse was not dead. He was very much alive. He still drove his car. If you saw him, you would not know that he had cancer, but he was consumed with anger.

I advised my coworker to tell her cousin to focus on living, remove the anger and God may extend more years on his life. I also asked her to tell her cousin to try to and see his wife's view of her marriage. His wife was a younger woman who loved him. A younger woman who said for better or worse, sickness and in health but was not prepared for the better or worse or sickness and in health. She too was also angry. She said, I Do, but in her reality she was saying I Don't or I love you too much too see you die. I told my co-worker to her cousin to have a little empathy and sympathy for his wife. Love her through her emotional turbulence. Throw your pride away. The weather is bad, but it will change. I prayed for him as well. Shoot, his wife was probably chilling by herself. I know how to chill by myself. I went to the Bahamas had a wonderful time. I met other single women who were going through something, knew their worth, valued herself and jumped on a plane. I even met a few couples. The husband would act as our chaperon. So much fun

Nutrition Get up every day with a grateful heart. Live with joy. Continue an intimate, romantic and sexual relationship with your spouse. Pray for strength, healing, joy and wisdom..

It's essential for both spouses to seek counseling. Remember each person has free will as it is in accepting Jesus Christ. I had to seek counseling for me whether my spouse did or not. So do you. I pray you both choose counseling. Spouses were created to enjoy giving and receiving love. Some treatments are different for each marriage covenant, but there is a treatment.

We are living our dreams. Mr. Thomas Saunders Jr. and Mrs. Carol Overton Saunders, aka Mr. and Mrs. Thomas Saunders Jr.

Be open be honest with yourself and each other, especially with your counselor. Denial may lead to death or stress

In 2014 and 2015 I found out that M & M was a form of medicine and nourishment which keeps me sexually satisfied, married and healthy. I'm thankful for the reality of a past and present practice of mediation and masturbation, knowing my self-worth and self-care. I'm so thankful for exercise, medicine, prayer, meditation, worship and praise I appreciate my mentors to coaches to spiritual advisors, friends and family, inclusive of ancestors both biblical and heritage.

The woman behind her services and products, Queen2CHope -Me, is whole and well balanced. I am a woman, mother, friend and wife. I worship and praise God in all things.

Growing up I would say" M & M", meditation and masturbation. OMG, I never knew M & M would be one of my life supports.

No longer bound nor ashamed. No need to apologize for M & M. I am free to be me, Queen2CHope with an intimate relation with God.

Someone reading this book or listening to the audio may say that you'll get use to masturbation or you may prefer masturbation over the man or you won't appreciate the touch of your spouse I BEG TO DIFFER. Free to be me, Queen2CHope. As I am writing, I remember a song, "Last Night a DJ saved my life. In my life DJ stands for Dr. Rev Coach La Tonia for her Juicy Spirit Awakening coaching and counseling. Some men are not as "Awaken" as women. Whether your spouse is sick or not, you need Juicy Spirit Awakening. Ladies and Men. Especially ladies. "One will pursue pleasure, passion, purpose and partake a sensual spiritual immersion program." Dr. Rev Coach La Tonia Taylor-Bey

One of my Juicy Spirit sisters shared an article:

"10 Wicked Reasons You Should Be Masturbating More Often," which I will share with you shortly by Author Alexandria Jamieson.

There are so many spouses including single women, who are suffering in silence. There is no shame or embarrassment. Religion, customs, myths have been forms of restraints that have caused more harm than good.

I appreciate the benefits of medicine, exercise meditation worship and praise. So why should I not appreciate the benefits of masturbation!

ENTRIES FROM MY JOURNAL

Entry 1
Carol A, Overton Saunders Good Juicy Morning Don't look or wait for someone else to stimulate juicy sexual moments, travel, open a business or anything with or for you. You are an Eloquent Queen with vibration and energy

not to be ashamed of. Spread your legs in the nude exotic environment you create alone with self and let your heart & body feel alive. Remember that you are not dependent but independent while in a relationship.

Entry2

Marriage is Like Mashed Potatoes

> **To My Sister**
>
> Enough Already Sister:
>
> Let's talk about "The Divine Feminine" of you and me.
>
> Last year I was on a call for women entrepreneurs. The host presented a guest speaker, Rev. La Tonia Taylor-Bey, who delved into the Divine Feminine - "Juicy Spirit." I am so glad I was on the call.
>
> The Devine Feminine is no secret to you or me nor is it the forbidden fruit. How can you or I or our emotions be a secret to us. Shoot I refuse to be a slave to the world community, church community or husband. I am FREE to be ME. No more suffocation. I have abilities, a voice and feelings, especially sexual feelings that need healing. LOL. I'm thinking about the late Marvin Gaye's song Sexual Healing.
>
> My husband was ill and sex was down for a while. At first I thought I had to be down. Shoot my body was tired, and frustrated. But, if you looked at me you would never know. S_ _t, my Vagina was dry. Solo adventures increased. S_ _t after that call secret who, hush who and solo adventures took me to the Bahamas.
>
> Sis " Divine Feminine" is owning and owing you with no guilt, shame or disrespect to anyone.
>
> How the hell is sexual desire or pleasure sexual immorality then in the next breath moral please. Water is water. My feelings/desires are real.
>
> An awakening to the body and mind. Come out and play and enjoy you. Denial of self was hurting other areas of my life; business, creative ideas, dance, marriage. Yes marriage, I was resenting "for "sickness and in health." Hubby's sickness didn't contribute 100% to my lack of desire. I had a responsibility to be true to self and he was required to true to be himself. S_ _t my desire didn't develop when I met him. So Why should it stop when I'm with him.
>
> Sis wake up to you everyday. Please don't let world community, church community or marriage package your desire and ability in a box and shelf it. Sometimes as professionals, we just do what we do not even realizing we are is stupor – almost like a functioning addict.
>
> Life more Abundantly. Arise and Shine.
>
> I truly recommend Rebirth with , Rev. La Tonia Taylor-Bey

Here is the article I said I would share with you on Masturbation posted by <u>Alexandra Jamieson</u>on July 20, 2015 in <u>Conscious Sexualit y</u> <u>Secrets</u>:

The Author
Alexandra Jamieson is a functional nutrition coach, chef, and mom. She is the co-creator of the Oscar- nominated documentary Super Size Me, and the author of the new "self-health" book Women, Food & Desire. Alex has been seen on Oprah, Martha Stewart Living, CNN, Fox News, USA Today and People Magazine. Alex offers remarkably sane — and tasty advice on how to detox, live healthfully and feel fantastic. She lives in Brooklyn where she juggles, somewhat gracefully, raising her 8-year-old son, trying new gluten-free recipes, running her company and riding her bicycle to the food co-op.

Masturbation is both a powerful healer and an incredibly uncomfortable topic to talk about.

Yes, everyone masturbates!
And yes, we should also be doing it more.
According to Indiana University's National Survey Of Sexual Health And Behavior, more than half of American adults report masturbation between one and four times a week. Masturbation though has developed a bad reputation mainly because religion and culture tell us it's a sin.

As a result, many of us feel at least some trace of shame, guilt, or even fear when practicing this very natural act. *But with all it's incredible and scientifically proven benefits it's time to finally embrace masturbation!*

MUST READ: The Incredible Benefits Of Mutual Masturbation

10 Good Reasons To Make Masturbation A Habit

#1 It Makes You Relaxed

According to the 2009 University of Michigan study orgasms cause the body to release dopamine, endorphins and oxytocin (the "love and bonding" hormone).

The boost of these hormones in turn lowers cortisol, a main stress hormone. Chronically elevated cortisol levels lead to inflammation, stress-eating, insomnia, and weight loss resistance.

This means your pleasure-powered workouts will help lead to a toned body.

#2 It Makes You Eat Healthier

Higher levels of oxytocin make us feel happier, which keeps those emotionally triggered food cravings for sugar, cheese, and other "comfort foods" at bay.

Oxytocin levels are usually increased simply through the physical stimulation of the clitoris vagina, cervix, and breasts.

So, even if you don't reach climax, you'll still release this powerful neurotransmitter.

#3 IT IMPROVES SPERM QUALITY

Why? There is less DNA damage and fewer motility problems with fresh sperm.

#4 IT IS PHYSICALLY HEALING

The gut and the mind are inextricably linked. In my book *Women, Food, and Desire*, I tell the story of a client who wasn't dating, and wasn't masturbating.

She had been suffering from bloating, gas, and a frustrating "muffin top" that wouldn't budge for years. I introduced her to a regular self- pleasure routine.

After a couple of weeks of regular self-pleasure, she noticed a marked difference in her digestion, and her bloating had reduced greatly.

#5 IT MAKES YOU MORE SELF CONFIDENT

Masturbating leads to increased self-confidence and a positive upward spiral of self-care.

When you know what you need to bring yourself pleasure and orgasm, you strengthen your emotional intelligence and connection to your body.

Knowing how your body works and what you're capable of, regardless of your relationship status, helps you make better decisions and create stronger boundaries about dating and mating.

When you can bring yourself physical pleasure, you don't need someone else to validate that you're sexy. You know it.

MUST READ The Art Of Self Pleasure {4 Unique Ways To Pleasure Yourself}

#6 It Makes You Want More Sex
Another study reveals that sexy daydreams release testosterone in women.

This means that when you read erotic fiction, or watch any kind of port that excites you, your body will begin anticipating encounter, which naturally raises your libido and quite literally gets your juices flowing.

#7 It Makes You Feel Less Pain
Orgasms (and to a lesser extent simple sexual arousal) increase blood flow to both your brain and reproductive organs, which helps soothe menstrual cramps and headaches.

MUST READ: Painful Period? 6 Natural & Powerful Ways to Liberate Yourself from Period Pain

#8 It Is Kind Of Like Meditating
Sexual pleasure is a great way to clear your mind of excessive anxiety. It brings you to the present moment; kind of like meditating!

The physical release triggers stress relief and can be a great way to get in touch with your body (and out of your head).

Being in the moment, and focusing on what feels physically good to you, is a wonderful intentional practice with many benefits.

MUST READ: <u>5 Ways Meditation Will Help You Have Mind-Blowing Sex</u>

#9 It Keeps Your Sex Life Alive

Especially if you're single, or in a long-distance relationship, self-pleasure is a great way to help keep your sexual energy stay alive.

By self-stimulating you're keeping your reproductive tissues flexible, strong, and healthy. The more solo-sex you have, the more you'll want sex. This is really helpful for couples that are separated, and for singles looking to keep their sexual energy high.

#10 It Feels Awesome

Yes it does! and we all need more pleasure in our lives, am I right?

[By Alexandra Jamieson| Featured Artist: Franz von Bayros| Originally posted on <u>Mind Body Green</u> *Do you want more conscious sex, love & life secrets? Follow My Tiny Secrets*

<u>Facebook Twitter YouTube</u> Did you like the post? Make sure to share it with your friends.]

CHAPTER 9
Let Me Tell You

§

GOD WHO IS THE CREATOR of a potato and marriage is bigger than a potato and spouse. God is with His creation during the sun, rain, hail, snow and wind. God covers both potato and spouse during turbulence and harmonious seasons. God cares about all His creations. Remember there is someone bigger than you and your spouse. Spend some time with God. There are so many resources in the field of the Kingdom of God to assist you before, during and after the marriage; including the transition of your loving spouse to his or her. Heavenly home with God our Father.

In the garden, seeds are planted to grow vegetables, fruits and flowers.

In the garden man and woman were planted to grow and produce offspring.

In the garden unauthorize insects, animals and people enter. They trespass. They are unwanted and uninvited.

Pestilent: *destructive to life, deadly, causing annoyance, troublesome, harmful or dangerous to moral or public order, pernicious.*

In the garden we have to protect our vegetables, fruits, flowers and people.

Vegetables, fruits and flower are protected by insecticidal soap nontoxic sprays, which are harmless to them but toxic to unwanted and uninvited creatures

Vegetables, fruits and flowers are protected with Ortho Flower, Fruit & Vegetable Insect Killer Ready Spray. There are other sprays; I like Ortho products.

Man and woman are protected by accepting, believing and applying the Word of God. Cast down arguments and every high thing that exalts Itself against the knowledge of God, bringing every thought into captivity to the obedience of Christ. [2 Cor. 10:5]

Sickness, Diseases, Bugs, Lying, Adultery, Selfishness, Quietness, Deceit and Stealing. There is so much more. What's in your Garden to cast down and out?

Potato
    Man & Woman
        Correlation
        RELATIONSHIP With
        our Creator

            GOD

Refreshed
Ready For A Delicious Meal

North Carolina road trip to visit Apostle Angela: Laughter, Food, Prayer & Prophetic Word. 2015

Marriage is Like Mashed Potatoes

Dr. Vikki Johnson
#All Things Vikki #Soul Wealth Academy
#Intangible Prosperity September 2014

Sacred Sisters Soul Luxury and Mentoring Florida Weekend

Marriage is Like Mashed Potatoes

**4 Generations of Love & Advice 4Life
Grandmother ~ Mother & Daughter
VIP Lunch with Queen Oprah ~The Life you Want
Tour, Newark. New Jersey, September 2014**

A Word From My Husband - I Shall share

❧

"And the two shall become one." We should put no one before one another but God. Stop trying to be people pleasers and do what's pleasing to each other. Move self-gratification aside, the husband (me) should desire to do what makes the wife (you) happy and the wife (you) should feel likewise towards her husband (me), it's not about me, nor is it all about you, it's about us! Never take each other for granted for tomorrow is not promised. I love my wife, and I married her for better or worse, but there are times I feel as though I don't exist when she becomes preoccupied with everyone and everything else. I'm here and it's for you, try to understand that. It's our marriage and I don't want it wasted Friday August 19th, 2011
    Thomas Saunders Jr. **Pastor Thomas Saunders Jr.**

Revive Us Again

Revive Us Again
Lord, you were favorable to your land;
  you restored the fortunes of Jacob.
2 You forgave the iniquity of your people;
  you covered all their sin. *Selah*
3 You withdrew all your wrath;
  you turned from your hot anger.
4 Restore us again, O God of our salvation,
  and put away your indignation toward us!
5 Will you be angry with us forever?
  Will you prolong your anger to all generations?
6 Will you not revive us again,
  that your people may rejoice in you?
7 Show us your steadfast love, O
  Lord, and grant us your salvation.
8 Let me hear what God the Lord will speak,
  for he will speak peace to his people, to his saints;
  but let them not turn back to folly.
9 Surely his salvation is near to those who fear
  him, that glory may dwell in our land.

¹⁰ Steadfast love and faithfulness meet;
   righteousness and peace kiss each other.
¹¹ Faithfulness springs up from the ground,
   and righteousness looks down from the sky.
¹² Yes, the Lord will give what is
   good, and our land will yield its
   increase.
¹³ Righteousness will go before him
   and make his footsteps a way.

Psalm 85 (ESV)
The Holy Bible, English Standard Version Copyright © 2001 by <u>Crossway Bibles</u>, a publishing ministry of Good News Publishers.

Three Strand Cord

〜

HAVE YOU HEARD ABOUT THE "Three Strand Cord"?
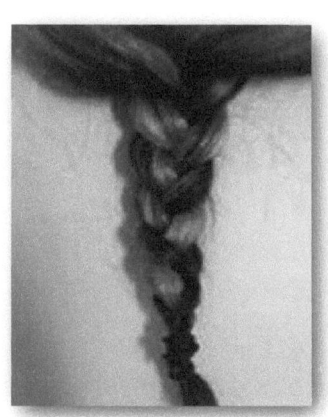
Here is my interpretation as it relates to the marriage covenant; Spouse to Spouse with Jesus Christ.

This is a combination of three groups of hair formed into a braid or cornroll. Not a twist. A twist normally has two strands of hair.

A three strand cord is a combination of three strands of hairs. My view of the cord: Each spouse is independently reaching to God who is the center of our lives. God wraps each spouse constantly. God's oil is received more upon the yielding of each spouse. Occasionally a spouse or both will display restraints to God's instructions. But God is always at work. Where is the oil? A three strands cord must constantly be wrapped [snugged] in oil. Don' let a strand stray. Stay wrapped and connected to God. Keep Him smack in the middle of your marriage

And we know that for those who love God all things work together for good, for those who are called according to his purpose. [Romans 8:28 ESV]

By yourself you're unprotected. With a friend you can face the worst. Can you round up a third? A three stranded rope isn't easily snapped. [Ecclesiastes 4:12 MSG]

Remember, "Mr. Potato Head and Mrs. Potato Head," the, "toy," consisting of a plastic model of a potato, which can be decorated with a variety of plastic parts that can attach to the main body? Well they are toys we are real. Allow God through His son Jesus Christ the work of the Holy Spirit to change you from the inside out. The Potato Head toy has interchangeable parts. Spouses, have a heart and mind that can be changed into the image of Jesus Christ. We can be washed and cleaned by the blood of Jesus Christ.

Marriage is like mash potatoes. Unfortunately, there are some rotten potatoes which must be thrown away. A potato, spouse or both spouses become rotten when it or they refuse nourishment from our savior Jesus Christ for a delicious creamy savoring mash potato meal for life.

You can't just receive Jesus Christ. You must receive His nutrients which are His instruction, seasoning and love. You must also do what is required to be and have a delicious meal 4Life. Essential nourishment is found in the Word of God.

Taste and see that the Lord is good. Be a doer of the Word. I don't like throwing away food. Jesus Christ is a wonderful counselor. Many are called but few are chosen. Will you taste and see that the Lord is good?. Will you let Jesus into your marriage?

Prayer: Father God I pray for the individual(s) reading your message in Marriage is Like Mash Potatoes; I pray that he or she will do and be all that you require of him or her for marriage and beyond. **In Jesus Name**

Carol's Daughter of God Inspirational Cards

Other Books by Carol

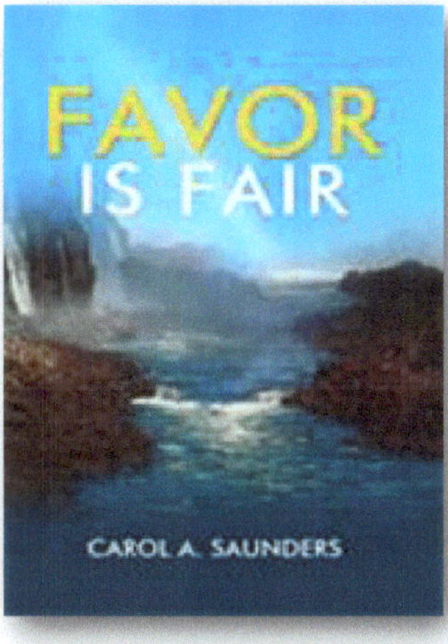

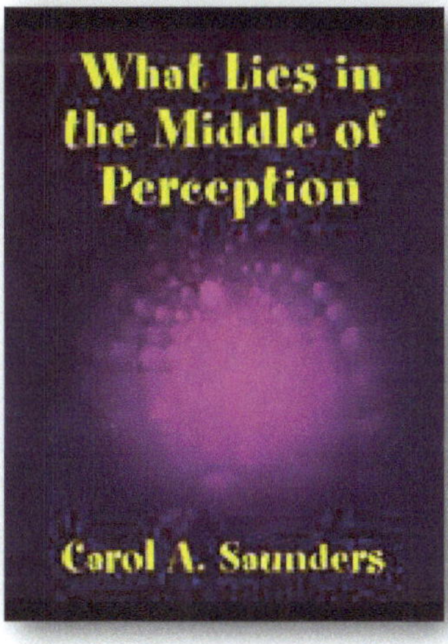

Stay in Touch w/ Me

§

Facebook
  Carol Saunders Enterprises

Look for the audio of "Marriage is like Mash Potatoes:
April 2016

Appreciation

I APPRECIATE ALL THE INGREDIENTS I receive from my relationship with God, my creator, his son Jesus Christ and Holy Spirit.

One morning while I was sitting outside, I thought about some child thoughts about marriage and then what I thought about marriage as an adult looking at couples. Thank God I kept looking to Him.

Feeling thankful

I WANT TO THANK:

Me, Queen2CHope, Carol A. Overton Saunders: for being honest, seeking help and doing the work to become a better me, friend and marital partner 4Life.

My husband, Thomas Saunders Jr., for doing the work to become a better him, friend and marital partner 4Life.

Thank you so much Queen Shenetta Malkia Sapp, my daughter/best friend, for your love and support. No Bullying. Empowerment Essence.com

Dr. Vikki Johnson, mentor/friend. Sisterhood, spiritual, professional and emotional assistance Soul Wealth Academy http://www.vikkijohnson.com/#!soul-wealth-academy/c1nok

Apostle Angela Thomas, By His Spirit World Mission: Prophetic words & prayers for singles/ couples, spiritual, sisterhood and professional assistance. Spiritual Motherhood;

Rev Coach La Tonia Taylor-Bey: www.rebirthinternational.net;

Rev Malinda Euell, Thema Azize Serwa, Womb Sauna Therapy;

Apostle Tresti Cunningham, Eternal Life in Christ Ministries, Inc. Prophetic words 2me 2014 and prayers for couples;

My Sacred sisters, Soul Wealth Academy and Juicy Butterflies-Goddesses

Intercessors Chantia Simmons, Pastor Tammy McNair, Minister Sandra Chaney, Evelyn Williams, Minister Monique Simmons, Rev. Juanita Gonzalez, Rev Kim Queen and Minister Lejeune Farmer;

Thank you married couples who are living and fulfilling God's plan for marriage. You encourage me;

Thank you to my Single Sisters and Brothers who encourage me to be a free spirit, stay beautiful & true to myself; to remember my worth and value;

Thanks Mom, Rosemary Hamilton Overton and Dad, Noah Overton. Divorced yet believe in the marriage covenant

Thank you CreativeSpace.com Your commitment to excellence is truly appreciated. My team is Awesome.

Thank you Abba my Heavenly Father

#Queen2CHope
#Soaring
#Soaring High
#Message in the Arts
#Marriage Support

Resources

§

WORDS THAT BRUISE HOW TO know you're in an emotionally abusive marriage. © 2013 Focus on the Family (Canada) Association. All rights reserved

The Emotionally Destructive Relationship, Author Leslie Vernick

Jennifer Smith UnveiledWife.com, a a web-based ministry
Connect with Jennifer on social media @unveiledwife!
Husband and Wife for Life: www.HusbandandWifeforLife.com Mark and Laquilla Lane

Dr. Trenace Nicole Richardson: Real Women.: http://www.realwomenrock.org

Marriage Today: Jimmy & Karen Evans: http://www.marriagetoday.com

Black and Married with Kids: http://blackandmarriedwithkids.com

Joyce Meyer Ministries: https://www.joycemeyer.org.

References

THE HOLY BIBLE, ENGLISH STANDARD Version. Copyright ©2001 by Crossway Bibles, a publishing ministry of Good News Publishers. ible.info.

Holy Bible, New International Version®, NIV® Copyright © 1973, 1978, 1984, 2011 by Biblica, Inc.® Used by permission. All rights reserved worldwide

Anne Graham Lotz, The Bible Is Crystal Clear on Gender Equality - Woman may not fare well in world religions, but she is greatly loved by God who created her equal to man. http://www.faithstreet.com/onfaith/2007/01/17/biblical-record-is-clear-god- c/737

Max Lucado "God created marriage no government subcommittee envisioned it. no social organization developed it marriage was conceived and born in the mind of God."

"Words that bruise: How to know you're in an emotionally abusive marriage." Focus on the Family (Canada) Association.

Jennifer Smith UnveiledWife.com, a web-based ministry.

"You stiff-necked people! Your hearts and ears are still uncircumcised. You are just like your ancestors: You always resist the Holy Spirit!
LOL.: Laugh Out Loud

One Potato Two Potato not three Potato Four

About the Author

Advocate and Giver of Inspirational Hope.
Covers in prayer and law individuals in a committed relationship and covenant marriage
She assist in changing and correcting a wrong by staying current and involved with people, communities and world events.
Carol A. Overton Saunders: Professional Paralegal with over 32 years of experience with the Department of Justice.

Volunteer in Correctional Facilities: Program facilitator of Parenting classes; Empowerment thru the Arts classes and Board member, Women Moving Forward Project, National Association of Women Judges [criminal recidivism]

She is an author, inspirational speaker, preacher, professional dancer, entrepreneur & traveler

What's unique about Her?

Her creativity in the arts, Crazy Faith; dedication and services as a paralegal. She is loyal, trustworthy and won't compromise her integrity as a person Mother or Wife

www.ingramcontent.com/pod-product-compliance
Lightning Source LLC
Chambersburg PA
CBHW042308150426
43198CB00001B/8